This book is dedicated to all who find Nature not an adversary to conquer and destroy, but a storehouse of infinite knowledge and experience linking man to all things past and present. They know conserving the natural environment is essential to our future well-being.

DEVILS TOWER
THE STORY BEHIND THE SCENERY®

by Stephen Norton

STEPHEN NORTON, a graduate of Northern Michigan University, served as a seasonal interpreter at Devils Tower National Monument for several years. Steve taught high school English at Hulett, Wyoming, just nine miles from the Tower.

Devils Tower National Monument *located in northeastern Wyoming, was proclaimed America's first national monument in 1906 to preserve this 867-foot tower of columnar rock.*

Front cover: Devils Tower bathed in sunlight, photo by Larry Ulrich. Inside front cover: Playful young black-tailed prairie dogs, photo by Glenn Van Nimwegen. Page 1: Northern oriole, photo by Erwin & Peggy Bauer. Page 2/3: The Tower's forest foreground, photo by Ed Cooper.

Edited by Mary L. Van Camp • Book design by K. C. DenDooven.

Seventh Printing, 2010 • New Version

DEVILS TOWER: THE STORY BEHIND THE SCENERY © 1991 KC PUBLICATIONS, INC.

Theodore Roosevelt, although never setting an eye on the Devils Tower, recognized it as a scientific

wonder and proclaimed this magnificently columned
natural structure America's first national monument in 1906.

*Devils Tower—
a symbol held in
reverence by Native
Americans, a structure
that captured the
imagination of an
American president,
a source of challenge
and achievement
to the world's climbers,
and a spectacle that
elicits feelings of awe
and astonishment from
all its visitors. This
mass of rock stands
1,267 feet above
the Belle Fourche River
that freed it from the
layers of earth that
once enveloped it. It
has been here for some
50 million years.*

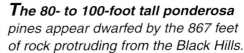

The 80- to 100-foot tall ponderosa
pines appear dwarfed by the 867 feet
of rock protruding from the Black Hills.

The Devils Tower Story

DICK DIETRICH

Like golden fingers reaching into the sky, the Tower is actually a marvelous example of geologic process, the very slow cooling of molten magma.

Devils Tower National Monument is visited by over 400,000 people each year, and countless others have witnessed it in the movie, "Close Encounters of the Third Kind." Viewing the rock is an enlightening personal experience.

Weathering has sent many of the Tower's columns crumbling to its base, and its cracks and wrinkles have worn deep. Yet, what has aged has done so graciously, leaving a stunning tribute to all of our nation's natural wonders.

America has only so many of these natural treasures, so we, as National Park Service rangers, as United States citizens, and as appointed caretakers to our own planet have a supreme duty and obligation to look out for all of our spectacular, most senior citizens. And as we exercise care, so rolls by another 560 million years that the Devils Tower National Monument will continue to stand bold in the West.

Along the Belle Fourche River, this mallard and her ducklings feed by tipping forward in the river's shallow edge. This species of duck is seen in the park throughout the summer.

LARRY BURTON

The groundsel is found along most of the paths away from the Tower itself.

LARRY BURTON

WES CARROLL

In winter, the prairie dogs are active above ground on the warmer days. They rely primarily on their fat stores accumulated throughout the summer and fall for food.

From this vantage point comes
a clear view of the Tower's multisided columns
that appear to catch the sun's rays and
hurl them toward spectators in
a fascinating combination of golden hues.

The Tower

Rising majestically out of a forest of towering ponderosa pines, the Devils Tower stands tall, boasting its claim as America's first national monument. Travelers are generally awestruck by their first far-off glimpse of the Tower as they approach it from the highways, yet once at its base, they gain a perspective of this imposing rock formation, the largest of its kind in the United States.

Devils Tower, with all its immensity, doesn't evoke an ominous or foreboding reaction from its visitors. The splendor, the color, and the docile surroundings leave all that view it with a peaceful feeling. Rather than imagining the gunfights of the Wild West, one pictures the rhythmic dance of its Indian brothers or the slow movement westward of the settlers who used the Tower as a landmark.

THE TOWER HAS MANY FACES

A look at each of those faces is easily captured through a leisurely one-and-a-quarter mile walk around its base. As you leave the visitor's center, a paved path winds uphill to the Tower Trail that encircles the monument once called "Mato Tipila" (Bear Lodge) by the Indians.

From this vantage point comes a clear view of the Tower's multisided columns that appear to catch the sun's rays and hurl them toward spectators in a fascinating combination of golden hues. If one stood here throughout the day, the sun's movement and the shadows of passing clouds would enchant the viewer with various shades of red, yellow, salmon, and rust; yet this can easily be captured simply by moving up the Tower Trail into the boulder fields.

Many amateur climbers will work the boulder field as a source of recreation. These large pieces of fallen columns encircle the Tower and can be reached directly from the Tower Trail.

CATHERINE GOCKLEY

These boulders were once part of the Tower itself. Through countless years of wear from the elements, shelves and fissures formed in the Tower's sides as some columns came crashing down. Some of these large sections that you touch right from the trail are approximately 8 feet in diameter and reach lengths of 25 feet.

TOM & PAT LEESON

One must never be so captivated by the Devils Tower that they miss much of the natural setting which it overlooks. The Black Hills of Wyoming and South Dakota hold a special beauty all their own. The trees in sunset lend a brilliance to this forest.

Breaking through the boulder field leaves visitors with ponderosa pines as their neighbors. These adult pines, many at 150 to 180 feet tall, give a true measure of the full 867 feet of the rock shaft. Sometimes dizzied at the height, visitors will turn away from the Tower where they are met by another form of elegance. Four hundred feet below, the Belle Fourche River, the subtle sculptor of Devils Tower, winds through the gentle hills of northeast Wyoming. Yet a mysterious hand pulls them away from this and draws them further down the path into the shadow of the weathered giant.

A glimpse from this side reveals many of the most popular climbing routes up the Tower. Men and women work ropes, wedges, and chocks like industrious ants scaling a wicker picnic basket. Once again we are given an idea of the size of the rock as climbers toil inside the fissures, while inching their way up.

Continuing around, the path turns away from the Tower and leaves us time to consider how it was actually formed.

FORMATION OF THE TOWER

The formation of Devils Tower occurred in the early Tertiary Period some 50 million years ago. Geologists believe that a mass of molten rock forced its way up through miles of rock, forming an inverted, cone-shaped structure under the strong layers of shale, gypsum, sandstone, and limestone that make up most of what is now northeastern Wyoming.

With these upper layers blanketing the molten magma, it was forced to cool slowly into a granite-like rock known as *phonolite porphyry.* That same slow cooling process cracked and fractured the rock in a honeycomb pattern that resulted in perhaps the most significant aspect of the Tower—the multisided columns that cover the entire circumference of the rock.

The climbing done on Devils Tower only adds to the mystique of the rock. Thousands of climbers each year come to this haven where the vertical cracks offer unique climbing opportunities.

JENNIFER ADAMS

These vertical columns formed around the central portion of the Tower only, although many extend the length of the mass' great height.

A haven for rock-climbing enthusiasts, the columns radiate out at angles of 120 degrees to form six-sided columns. Because the cooling was not uniform throughout the mass, however, columns range from three- to eight-sided.

Still well below the surface, erosion set in to free the formation from the softer sedimentary rock. The primary agent in this erosion was the Belle Fourche River. It carried away the sedimentary layers, inch after inch, over millions of years to expose the igneous rock, which is much more resistant to erosion.

The solidified magma became more of a dome-shaped mass as the river worked the area around it. But the elements of rain, heat, cold, wind, and gravity set in to separate the fissures and eventually sent columns crashing down thereby giving the Tower the slender and pronounced shape we see today.

Now 1,267 feet above the river that freed it, the Tower stands 867 feet high. Its 800-foot diameter base tapers off to a flat, teardrop-shaped top that measures 450 feet north to south and 250 feet east to west.

The Tower appears to sit on a wooden hill, but this is actually the bottom of the unexposed magma which was covered with fallen columns and soil. The deep-rooted pines lend a more subtle look to the landscape from afar, yet the terrain around the base is somewhat steep and rocky.

Abruptly, the trail turns back toward the Tower, and in the intense afternoon sunlight, while the time-worn top of the Tower still looks gray and cold, a golden brilliance is captured by the remainder of the side.

Finally the trip has been completed as we make our way back toward the visitor center. Having looked at the Tower from all sides, only one question remains. It is the question most frequently asked of the park's employees: "What is on top of the Devils Tower?"

THE TOP OF THE TOWER

Our imagination leads us to believe that the top of this rock would simply look like the top of any rock—cold, barren, and void of anything special. The tower, however, is no ordinary rock! Its 1.5-acre area is not unlike much of the countryside around it.

Although it appears flat from below, the summit is actually humped with a few small outcroppings here and there. It is covered by grasses and other plants. The prickly-pear cactus, a hardy,

CATHERINE GOCKLEY

On a clear day, climbers reaching the Tower's summit can see four states—Wyoming, North Dakota, South Dakota, and Montana.

smaller cactus, is abundant and offers discomfort to many weary and unaware climbers.

Prairie sagewort also grow there, as does *Artemsia tridentata*—the native big sage. It is likely that seeds from these plants were deposited by the turkey vultures or the prairie falcons that nest in the upper portions of the columns.

All of these plants might seem plausible, but animals at the top would be seemingly impossible. Yet, animals are up there—rattlesnakes, pack rats, and least chipmunks have all been spotted. These animals work their way up the cracks and fissures of the Tower to the top.

As the sun fades over the horizon, the Tower takes on a final look to visitors who have ventured the base trail. The look is no longer warm and inviting, but harsh and cold as the Tower stands a dark, lonely sentinel overlooking the Black Hills.

SUGGESTED READING

TRIMBLE, DONALD E. *The Geologic Story of the Great Plains*. Theodore Roosevelt. Roosevelt Nature and History Association, 2001.

ROBINSON, CHARLES S. *Geology of Devils Tower*. Devils Tower Natural History Association, 1981.

And, just as it emerges from this morning mist, Devils Tower was freed from the layers of sedimentary rock that surrounded it. The Tower is made up of an igneous rock called "phonolite porphyry," which is nearly as dense as granite. The erosive forces that worked away at the area over time had relatively little effect on the Tower itself, save for the fallen columns that make up the boulder field.

The Geologic Experience

On seeing the Devils Tower for the first time, visitors usually envision thoughts of a violent upheaval in which this huge rock forced its way through the earth's layers and thrust out in a dramatic and powerful fashion. However, the formation of the Tower was a gradual process that began with a mass of molten magma trapped within the earth's crust. After that magma cooled and hardened, erosion became the principal force that would expose the rock, with an ancestor of the Belle Fourche River doing most of the work.

During the earth's Tertiary Period approximately 50 million years ago, magma forced its way up into the surrounding sedimentary rock layers.

As the magma cooled, cracks developed and the rock fractured into multisided columns. Over millions of years, erosion worked away at the softer sedimentary rock around this formation, and the Devils Tower was slowly uncovered.

GEORGE WUERTHNER

***M**ost of the erosion of*
the earth surrounding the
Tower was washed away by what is now known as the Belle Fourche River.
The effect of this river, which flows on the southern border and then cuts through
the park, have greatly diminished. Dams and reservoirs upriver control the slow,
steady flow of what looks like a stream today. The red siltstone bordering the river
provides a sharp contrast here, and the carved walls illustrate the power of water erosion.

Challenge of the Rock

The upper third of the Tower is much more worn than the lower two-thirds. This section has been exposed to the elements much longer in the erosion process. The cracks, both vertical and horizontal here, run deep and jagged. The effects of ice, rain, wind, and cold have loosened much of this area, and climbers must exercise extreme caution as the handholds and footing are treacherous. Possibly the next major rockfall will come from this area.

WES CARROLL

WES CARROLL

Climbers on this column give an indication of just how huge the Tower really is. Climbing in its weathered ranks, these humans seem quite minute while working their way, hand over hand, up 1- to 6-inch cracks for nearly 500 to 600 feet. They are grasping literally thousands of tons of rock as each column may span 12 feet across. And, as they move one foot up, one can only imagine the amount of time it took to expose that single foot of the Tower from its home beneath the northeastern Wyoming soil. So look closely at this picture—and wonder!

Although it appears flat from below, the summit is actually humped with a few small outcroppings here and there. It is covered by grasses and other plants.

The top is more than simply solid rock. It is actually its own little life zone. The one and one-half acres are home to several varieties of plant life. Prickly-pear cactus, big sage, and currant grow here amongst the rock outcroppings. Even a few animals venture on a journey to the top—snakes, chipmunks, field mice, and wood rats have been spotted there by climbers. These tiny animals work their way up in the same cracks used by their human counterparts.

GLENN VAN NIMWEGEN

LARRY ULRICH

Winter at Devils Tower is a quiet, yet brilliant season that only a handful of visitors generally witness. A hush falls over the grounds as well as a light snowfall that accents the cracks and fissures of the Tower's walls. Yet climbers might still venture here. Winter climbs have even taken place on Christmas and New Year's Day.

The sunlit tops of the ponderosa pine clash with the changing colors of the bur oak and the ash in autumn. As the chill hits in the crisp October afternoons, the Tower seems to loom taller and takes on a grayer face. The changing countryside bustles with activity as animals ready for winter and park visitation slowly drops off.

*D*odge was fascinated by what local Indians called Mato Tipila. His interpreters misunderstood and referred to this massive rock as "the bad god's tower." The name was modified and Dodge called it "Devils Tower" in his book **The Black Hills.**

Before There Was a Park

Prior to the 1600s, not much is known of the role of man and his association with the Devils Tower. Indians who roamed the plains—principally the Arapaho, Cheyenne, Crow, Kiowa, Shoshone, and Sioux—passed on many legends of the Tower. Some of these legends dealt with the many gods and spirits of the elements; thus the Tower was given many names. It was not until the late 1800s that the white man took a real interest in both the Black Hills area and this unusual rock formation.

When a U.S. Government geological survey party went out to map the Black Hills region in 1875, their military escort was headed by Colonel Richard I. Dodge. He was fascinated by what local Indians called Mato Tipila, but his interpreters misunderstood and referred to this massive rock as "the bad god's tower." The name was modified and Dodge called it "Devils Tower" in his book *The Black Hills*.

ESTABLISHING THE MONUMENT

Through the next decade, settlers moved into the region and established homesteads. Then in 1892, at the settlers' request, Wyoming Senator Francis E. Warren introduced a bill to preserve Devils Tower as a national park area. Although the bill never passed, Washington's General Land Office did keep a small area around the Tower from private ownership.

Fourteen years later, after Congress passed the Antiquities Act which was meant to preserve both scientific and man-made wonders, President Theodore Roosevelt, on September 24, 1906, established the Devils Tower National Monument as America's first national monument.

For the proper care and management of the monument, only 1,153 acres were set aside at that time. Congressional legislation added additional acreage for the establishment of camping and picnic areas in 1955. Today the park's area is 1,347 acres.

LARRY BURTON

Native Americans used the roots of the arrowleaf balsamroot for medicinal purposes. Its single flower wilts in the summer heat, but the foot-long leaves are evident through the fall.

KENT & DONNA DANNEN

Directly outside of the park this log structure, now in ruins, was originally a dance hall for area ranchers. Two such ranchers, William Rogers and Willard Ripley, were the first to climb the Tower in 1893.

THE FIRST CLIMB TO THE SUMMIT

As a bid for the preservation of Devils Tower was being waged, a plan to make the first climb to the summit was put into motion. Local ranchers William Rogers and Willard Ripley planned a spectacular Fourth of July celebration in 1893. For months, they planned a route up the south face.

Together they fashioned numerous thirty-inch stakes which were driven into a continuous vertical crack between two columns. Portions of this ladder can still be viewed today along the Tower Trail.

As the event drew near, Rogers and Ripley distributed handbills declaring that their feat would be "the rarest sight of a lifetime." The handbills also offered such amenities as food and drink daily and

nightly dancing, and plenty of hay and grain for the horses. The stunt had a financial purpose also as Mrs. Rogers was the entrepreneur who would be the concessioner.

As the Fourth came, over 1,000 spectators, some driving buckboards over 100 miles, arrived for the event and witnessed the climbers make the ascent in about one hour. To their surprise, Rogers then erected a flagpole which the two had placed on the summit earlier. On this, they hung a giant replica of Old Glory, which was later cut into pieces and sold as souvenirs.

NPS PHOTO

Fritz Weissner was the first free climber of Devils Tower. His 1937 climb marks the beginning of climbing records kept at the monument's administration building.

Among those visitors was Fritz Wiessner, a mountain climber, who in 1937 completed the first ascent of Devils Tower without the aid of the stake ladder. A year later, Jack Durrance discovered the "Durrance Route," today's most popular and the easiest of the Tower's summit climbs.

A DARING RESCUE

Durrance probably didn't plan to, but he would eventually return to make a daring rescue. In 1941, George Hopkins, a professional parachutist, boasted that he could land at the top of the Tower, then descent with the aid of a 1,000-foot rope. Unbeknownst to the National Park Service, Hopkins made the jump successfully. Unfortunately, the rope for his escape was dropped and became entangled in the rock columns on the west face.

Hopelessly stranded, Hopkins settled in to let others figure a way to get him down. Claude Ice, a local pilot, was enlisted to do a number of food drops

After this initial celebration, the Tower became a popular place for annual Fourth of July picnics by local ranchers and their families who seldom saw each other the rest of the year. At the 1895 event, using her husband's ladder, Mrs. Rogers became the first woman to climb to the top of the Tower.

Through all of this, Devils Tower never really became a tourist attraction. Because no passable roads or a bridge were established, very few people visited before 1920. Then in 1921, Crook County Commissioner John M. Thorn was appointed as the custodian of the monument by the National Park Service. Gradually, improvements were made that included a more passable road, a log shelter for visitors and, in 1928, a bridge across the Belle Fourche River.

The 1930s began an era of marked improvement for visitors to the Tower. A full-time custodian was appointed to oversee development of the land. Using labor from the Civilian Conservation Corps (CCC), they constructed housing for employees, new roads, picnic and camping areas and, in 1935, a rough-hewn log museum that is today used as the visitor center. As a result, many thousands of visitors saw the park.

to Hopkins. In the meantime, park officials looked for solutions and were offered several options.

While Goodyear offered the services of a blimp and the Navy offered the yet untested helicopter, the Park Service decided on Jack Durrance as the most plausible means to rescue Hopkins. Durrance, with a number of other climbers, returned to the Durrance Route to end Hopkins' six-day ordeal.

A relative calm settled over Devils Tower National Monument after the Hopkins incident, and park attendance and Tower ascent figures continued to rise, hand in hand.

GALEN ROWELL—MOUNTAIN LIGHT

From the air, the tear-drop shape of the Tower's top is disclosed. At approximately 300 feet from north to south and 180 feet from east to west, it is about the size of a football field. Although it appears flat from the ground, the domed shape of the summit is evident here.

> *Climbing enthusiasts deem it as some of the best crack rock climbing in the world, and they return each year to make a more difficult climb.*

INTO THE NATIONAL SPOTLIGHT

In 1977, Devils Tower was pushed into the national spotlight as the setting for a spaceship landing in the hit movie "Close Encounters of the Third Kind." Millions of Americans viewed the film and curiosity set in. Many believed that the Tower didn't exist, but was the work of Hollywood special effects personnel. As the word got out that this natural oddity was real, the monument's attendance rates skyrocketed. For quite some time, the most frequent question became, "Now, where did the spaceship land?"

Soon, the commotion over the motion picture died down, and today the 400,000 yearly visitors are in awe of the Tower for its own dramatic presence and not as the setting for an imaginary spaceship landing.

CLIMBING THE TOWER

Of all the visitors, about 1% have special memories of climbing the Tower. Climbing enthusiasts deem it as some of the best crack rock climbing in the world, and they return each year to make a more difficult climb.

There are over 220 routes up the sides of the Tower. Jack Durrance, before his rescue of George Hopkins, established the easiest route known as the Durrance Route in 1938. Other routes, some extremely difficult, should be reserved for expert climbers.

The only requirement that monument officials ask of climbers is to register before climbing, then to check out upon return. Safety, therefore, is in the hands of the individual, and rock climbers take many precautions. In the history of Devils Tower climbing, there has been only five fatalities. More injuries occur when visitors scramble through the boulder field, than with technical rock climbers.

On the average, it takes approximately 6 hours to climb, then repel down. One expert, however, started up a route and then appeared at the summit in just over 18 minutes!

Although climbing does play a part in the overall erosion of the Tower each year, the effect the climbers have is far less than the toll taken by the winter cold and summer heat.

PROTECTING THE MONUMENT

Devils Tower National Monument was established as our nation's first national monument because of its scientific and geological importance. Since that time, there has been a growing awareness of the Tower as a cultural resource. The Devils Tower Climbing Management Plan specifies a voluntary climbing closure during June—a month when American Indians participate in traditional cultural activites in the park. As a demonstration of respect for this sacred site, the National Park Service and American Indian tribes request that visitors observe this voluntary closure.

People come to the Tower for many reasons. For some people, the Tower is a fascinating geologic formation. To others, it is a sacred place. And for still others, it is a place for recreation. For nearly everyone, Devils Tower is a special place.

Today's monument staff is dedicated to balancing the educational, spiritual, and recreational values of Devils Tower while protecting the monument's natural and cultural resources.

SUGGESTED READING

GARDINER, STEVE AND DICK GUILMETTE. *Devils Tower National Monument Climbing Handbook.* Seattle: The Mountaineers Press, 1986.

MATTISON, RAY. *History of Devils Tower.* Devils Tower Natural History Association, 2000.

RAY ATKESON

At any time of the day, the view of the Tower has changed a bit. Light and shadows move up and down appearing to alter the shape, color, and size of each column. Climbers, once easy to spot working their way within a crack, seem to disappear as passing clouds block the sunlight.

Overleaf: *The Belle Fourche River carves its way through the park. Photo by Dick Dietrich.*

Looking down from the summit onto the Devils Tower visitors center must give climbers a feeling of accomplishment.

To The Top

Each day throughout the season, visitors can watch teams of climbers working the many routes. These climbs are technical in that climbers place equipment along their route to protect them in a fall. The average climb to the summit takes 4 to 6 hours.

CATHERINE GOCKLEY

By running their ropes through bolts permanently affixed to the Tower's walls, climbers can rappel down the side. With 165-foot ropes, they must complete 3 rappels to reach the bottom on the most common route. Rappelling off the summit usually takes from 30 minutes to an hour.

Climbers must register before, and immediately after, climbing each day. Registration is used for climber safety and also becomes part of a historical database that has been maintained since 1937.

The forces of nature create visual effects from a brilliantly blue sky to a menacing storm mood. Some benefit photographers; others spell caution for climbers.

JENNIFER ADAMS

GLENN VAN NIMWEGEN

The skies turn dark quickly as afternoon thunderstorms rush across the prairie to shower down upon the monument. Climbers must pay careful attention to rapidly changing weather patterns or they might be pummeled by a hail storm, drenched by rain, or buffeted by high winds.

Geological studies of the boulders and the lichen growing on the Tower, or on fallen columns, show that the last major fall here occurred some 10,000 years ago. These columns, many up to 25 feet long and 8 to 12 feet wide, cover the Tower's base and are known as the boulder field. They blanket the base and protect it against further erosion. The boulder field is also a source of recreation for visitors. Scrambling around on the rocks gives one a true appreciation of the sheer size of the Tower. Climbing beyond the field, however, requires registration with park officials.

The black-tailed prairie dog, the prevalent animal of the park, is somewhat responsible for many other species in the grasslands life zone. Predators are very active here.

Life Around the Tower

In sharp contrast to the barren stone of the Tower itself, the remaining 1,200 acres of the park are a haven for plants and animals. The gray Tower face, the seemingly fruitless prairie, the deep green of the forest, and the lazy blue of the Belle Fourche River create an abundance of opportunity to view several aspects of nature.

In such a small area by park standards, it is really quite amazing to experience the variety of habitats. In order to study each, it is necessary to label them as distinct "life zones." Each life zone is clearly defined by its plant life, and wildlife rarely roams from one to another. The Tower's life zones include the prairie grassland, the riverside woodlands, the ponderosa pine forest, and the rock shelves and fissures of the monument.

PRAIRIE DOG TOWN

The black-tailed prairie dog, the most prevalent animal of the park, dominates the grasslands life zone. In what is called "Prairie dog town" near the park entrance, these animals industriously excavate intricate burrows. The burrow network features a plunge hole that is marked by a low mound of dirt and sand, a nesting chamber where females give birth each spring, and a safety hole so they have an escape hatch if a predator entraps the animal and then pursues it.

Visitors see the prairie dogs sitting up outside of the plunge hole, and as tourists approach, the rodents give a quick, shrill bark, then disappear into the burrow.

The prairie dog is somewhat responsible for many other species in the grasslands life zone. Predators are very active here. The enemies include a

GLENN VAN NIMWEGEN

Black-tailed prairie dogs live in large colonies or "towns."

- 30 -

Nature not only abounds on the park's surface, but also beneath the waters of the Belle Fourche. Catfish, suckers, carp, minnows, and smallmouth bass live in the slow-moving water. These attract several of nature's fishermen including the kingfisher and the golden and bald eagles. Denning along the bank are foxes, raccoons, and muskrats. Thus the river supports a great deal of life on its own.

variety of hawks and eagles as well as bullsnakes, coyote, red fox, and mink.

In a scene often played out on the monument grounds, a red-tailed hawk circles high above the colony. The prairie dogs, basking in the warm midday sun, are distracted by a passing automobile. At this moment, the hawk plunges toward the ground picking out a victim who has strayed from the opening of its den. As a warning bark rings out, the "dogs" scurry for their holes, yet one never makes it, a victim of the hawk's powerful grip. And so another natural saga is played in the grasslands.

Prairie dog town is not the only grassland area of the Tower grounds, however. Visitors gain another look while hiking the Joyner Ridge Trail. On this 1.5 mile trail north of the Tower, hikers pass sandstone outcroppings and enter into meadows framed by deciduous trees and then move onto the prairie once more.

The needlegrasses and western wheatgrass dominate the soft slopes but splashes of color abound. Purple coneflowers, yarrow, sego lilies, and sunflowers dot the region and provide a picturesque setting where white-tailed deer and mule deer wander. The thirteen-line ground squirrel, a relative of the prairie dog, feeds on various seeds near its own burrow. Above it all fly the kings of the sky—turkey vultures are a real treat to watch as they use the air currents to scan the countryside for food.

RIVER AND WOODLANDS

The plains cottonwood, the state tree of Wyoming, is housed in the river and woodlands life zone. They stand on the banks of the Belle Fourche River and are home for many of the 90 species of birds that have been sighted at the park. The "rat-tat-tat" of the redheaded woodpecker rings out at all times of the day, and the swift black-capped chickadee hops from branch to branch, often feeding upside down in the American plums that settlers may have used in their own fruit preserves.

The river area is also home to the common grackle, the northern oriole, and the belted kingfisher. The kingfisher preys on minnows and frogs located near the banks. Mammals can be found along the banks of the Belle Fourche also. The most common is the white-tailed deer grazing on the bank's soft grasses, but the muskrat, beaver, and the raccoon are also occasionally spotted.

The porcupine, another nocturnal animal, enjoys feeding on the soft, yellow layer of cambium just under the bark of the ponderosa pine. They help to thin out the forest by eliminating dense tree growth.

MICHAEL H. FRANCIS

THE PINE FOREST

The most noticeable of the life zones is the pine forest. The Black Hills that rise like an oasis on the Northern Plains got their name from the deep green color of the trees and the shadows that they cast. From a distance, the hills literally look black.

ERWIN & PEGGY BAUER

The northern oriole, like many other birds, are easily distinguished by sex. The male is a brilliant, showy bird with orange-black markings while the female totes fewer colors.

DICK DIETRICH

The grasslands abound with animals, birds, and wildflowers. As a food for many wandering deer and other animals, the grasses serve as a nutritional staple, so the preservation of those grasses is crucial. Rangers keep tabs on weed growth so the native grasses aren't choked out.

CATHERINE GOCKLEY

This pine forest stands *at the foot of Devils Tower. Interspersed with the towering trees are huge boulders that have settled in beside the trees to blend in with the dark forest floor. These stones can provide havens for the woodland creatures.*

Because the ponderosas block so much sunlight, it is difficult for other inhabitants to become established. The quiet, cool, dark, and shady forest floors contain such plant varieties as the Oregon grape, harebell, and arrowleaf balsam root. The soil conditions here are quite poor because of the acids created by the pines. Only junipers hold up well to these conditions.

The forest area is not home to many animals. One who flourishes here though is the porcupine, one of the most misunderstood mammals. Porcupines do not throw their quills as many people believe. When threatened, they simply arch up and expose their enemy to 25,000 to 30,000 quills, then they strike out with their tails.

These nocturnal members of the rodent family help to keep nature's ecological balance by feeding on the inner bark of the pines, leaving many scars on the trees. But other than the porcupine, the forests may feature only red squirrels, some mice, and occasionally cottontail rabbits.

Birds don't abound in this coniferous forest either, but it is home to both the white- and red-breasted nuthatch, the pine siskin, the gray jay, and the dark-eyed junco.

TOM BEAN

Native western hares like *the jackrabbit are well adapted to prairie life.*

Living in the boulders at the base and sometimes seen at the top of the Tower, wood rats are industrious creatures that build nests in rock crevices.

LIFE ON THE TOWER

The final life zone is the Tower itself. The shelves and cracks are more than an area for climbers to rest and practice their art. Much of the color on the Tower is supplied by the brightly colored lichen that clings in yellow, green, and red. Orange star lichen, map lichen—which is usually bright yellow to yellow-green—and rock tripe lichen have the remarkable ability to grow where other plants simply can't.

Living up with the lichen are birds like the prairie falcon who nest in the rocks and hunt other birds or the inhabitants of prairie dog town. The rock dove or pigeon (usually associated with cities) is another bird who nests here. The gray birds blend well in the shadows and often surprise climbers by flapping out from the cracks.

Several members of the rodent family are full-time residents in the Tower's cliffs. The deer mouse, bushy tailed wood rat and least chipmunk all live in the rock crevices.

The red fox, adorned with a stunning coat, is rarely seen in the daylight. Survival for these small mammals depends upon their ability to hunt small rodents.

JOHN HENDRICKSON

Sunflower displays, from groundsel to daisies, add splashes of color to a dry countryside. These flowers flourish and spread across large areas from early June to August and enrich the grasslands.

NPS PHOTO

Geologists used the lichen—brightly colored areas on the rock—to date the last recorded rockfall from the Tower.

Complete with four zones, the park offers varied environments to its visitors. Unfortunately, many view the Tower as a pit stop between the two more celebrated parks, Mount Rushmore and Yellowstone, taking only an hour or two before motoring off.

Yet with recent improvements in the visitors service, the Devils Tower offers deer watching in the spring, playful prairie dogs in the summer, fall color changes splashed with spectacular rock outcroppings, and migrating eagles in the winter.

SUGGESTED READING

GUNDERSON, MARY ALICE. *Devils Tower: Stories in Stone.* Glendo, Wyoming: High Plains Press, 1988.

RATHBUN, SHIRLEY, ED. *First Encounters: Indian Legends of Devils Tower.* Belle Fourche, South Dakota: Sand Creek Printing, 1982.

SUGGESTED WEB SITES

www2.nature.nps.gov/views
www.devilstowerclimbing.com/
www2.nature.nps.gov/geology/parks/deto/
www.devils-tower.com

Prairie Dog Town

To protect all the others in the colony, prairie dogs will practice their characteristic "bark" to establish their territory. Principal enemies of the prairie dog include the rattlesnake, hawk, fox, coyote, and mink. Because some animals can follow them into their burrows, prairie dogs use an intricate series of tunnels throughout the town as escape routes.

TOM & PAT LEESON

JOHN P. GEORGE

Prairie dogs feed on most of the plants that grow within the colony's boundaries, thereby increasing visibility. Also, these plants are the primary water source for these critters.

ERWIN & PEGGY BAUER

Once the colony is alerted toward a possible danger, they rise up to spot the intruder or scramble quickly for their burrows. Cooperation is the main defense that the prairie dogs have.

Much of the grassland life tells us about the balance of life and the ways of nature. Observe: There is much more going on than just cute animals and pretty flowers

TOM & PAT LEESON

Grassland Life

Coyotes, year-round residents of northeastern Wyoming, prey on small rodents and animals. They sometimes enter the Tower grounds looking for an unsuspecting prairie dog.

Badgers burrow and tunnel after prairie dogs. These powerful carnivores grow up to two feet in length and can weigh up to twenty pounds.

ERWIN & PEGGY BAUER

Soaring high above the towns, red-tailed hawks can dive and grasp prey in only seconds.

Often mistaken for eagles in flight, the turkey vulture flies in slow, lazy circles near the top of Devils Tower. By holding their large wings slightly above horizontal, they work the wind's updrafts in search for dead animals.

Visitors need to be wary when approaching the prairie dog burrows. Rattlesnakes, like this prairie rattler are found in the monument and sometimes coil in the entrances of the dens.

This purple pasque flower can bear one or many stems and blooms in the early spring.

Flowers at Devils Tower

Numerous nature watchers comment that it is surprising to find such a quantity of wildflowers in the park's relatively small (1,347 acres) area. Hikers are treated to colorful blossoms flowering on the prairie, in the grasslands, under the forests, and even on the side of the Tower itself. Environmental conditions specific to each species allow for a variety with minimal rainfall, while differing blooming patterns give viewers a color change seemingly from week to week.

Prickly-pear cactus not only dot the park, but actually grow on the Tower. Climbers even encounter cactus at the summit.

One exotic in the park is the mullein (flannelflower). Its tightly packed yellow flowers bloom in the heat of summer.

Violet, bell-shaped flowers called harebells grow in amongst the boulders at the foot of the Tower.

The purple prairie clover flower throughout the summer on the open prairie.

The fruits of the chokecherry taste tart to downright sour, yet birds still feed here.

Red squirrels, the smallest of the tree squirrels, inhabit the coniferous forest. They are seen darting from tree to tree or among the rocks of the nearby boulder field.

MICHAEL H. FRANCIS

Spread throughout the coniferous forest directly surrounding Devils Tower are boulders that have tumbled beyond the boulder field. These huge stones lend a stabling presence to the area, yet also show that even the strongest in nature can become worn. Notice that the tree has shot up through what must have been a small fissure in the fallen rock, adding to the mystery. Numerous rocks dot the woods and become covered in lichen. They also become shelter for rodents and snakes, and contain pockets where rainwater is captured and used by birds.

CATHERINE GOCKLEY

The Forest

ERWIN & PEGGY BAUER

Marked by their yellow body and contrasting black wings, the American goldfinch is one of northeast Wyoming's native birds. Over 110 species of birds have been documented at Devils Tower.

JOHN HENDRICKSON

The American kestrel, formerly called the sparrow hawk, frequent the park grounds in the summer months. The smallest of the U.S. falcons, they are marked by a rich, reddish-brown on their backs, tails, and heads.

WES CARROLL

The Tower grounds sit at the westernmost edge of the bur oak trees' territory. They add grand color to the setting in autumn.

WES CARROLL

JOHN HENDRICKSON

***The* nocturnal raccoon frequents the monument** grounds. They are very opportunistic in their feeding habits, eating birds, crayfish, fruits, grains, small mammals, dead animals (carrion), and even insects!

***The* most frequently seen animal at Devils Tower is the white-tailed deer. Although they remain** deep in the forest shadows during the day, toward evening and again in the morning they can be seen in clearings throughout the park. The young are born each spring and hold onto their tell-tale white spots for four to five months. These browsers feed on most grasses and foliage. When feeling threatened, they turn to run and raise their foot-long tails, white underneath, like flags to signal their retreat.

ERWIN & PEGGY BAUER

***K*nown for their rapid** growth and heavy foliage, cottonwoods follow the Belle Fourche providing havens for numerous animals and birds. Redheaded woodpeckers, blue jays, orioles, and squirrels live in these trees, while white-tailed deer graze in the shade underneath.

WES CARROLL

The park *grounds, open year-round, have a number of trails that give visitors an opportunity to view the Tower from many vantage points.*

NPS PHOTO

Park staff *offer a variety of programs throughout the summer, giving visitors opportunities to learn about the different facets of the Tower.*

All About Devils Tower National Monument

DEVILS TOWER NATURAL HISTORY ASSOCIATION is a non-profit National Park Cooperating Association. Profits from Park Bookstore sales support interpretive and educational programs at the park. We invite you to join the Devils Tower Natural History Association and hope that you will stop at the Bookstore when you visit Devils Tower. The Association's bookstore is your best source for Devils Tower books and gifts. Visit their on-line catalog at: www.nps.gov/deto/bookshop.htm

RED SQUIRREL
MICHAEL H. FRANCIS

DEVILS

Junior Ranger

A Junior Ranger Program is available for children. Stop by the Visitor Center and pick up the Junior Ranger booklet. Once you complete the booklet, turn it in to a Ranger at the Visitor Center to receive the Junior Ranger Certificate.

TOWER

Contact Us

Devils Tower National Monument
P.O. Box 10
Devils Tower, WY 82714-0010

By Phone
(307) 467-5283

By fax
(307) 467-5350

Website
www.nps.gov/deto

A Tribal Narrative

Devils Tower stands as a symbol of strength and time to many of its visitors. To American Indians the Tower is a sacred place. Many tribal narratives explain the Tower's creation.

As a group of youngsters sought to become braves in their tribe, they came upon a huge grizzly. Their weapons useless, the children ran from the giant and scampered onto the top of a large rock. Realizing that the bear would soon be upon them, the children prayed to the spirits to save them.

The rock grew larger and larger as the bear approached, and as it sprung to grasp one child, the bear struck the side of the rock and slid down, its claws tearing away tons of rock. In the bear's fury, it leaped again and again at the children, each time ripping more grooves into the rock. At last, the bear realized that the efforts were futile, and he lumbered away.

This narrative, along with the stories of Rogers and Ripley, George Hopkins, and Close Encounters, add to the legend of Devils Tower, and we look forward to those events that will continue to provide bits of lore.

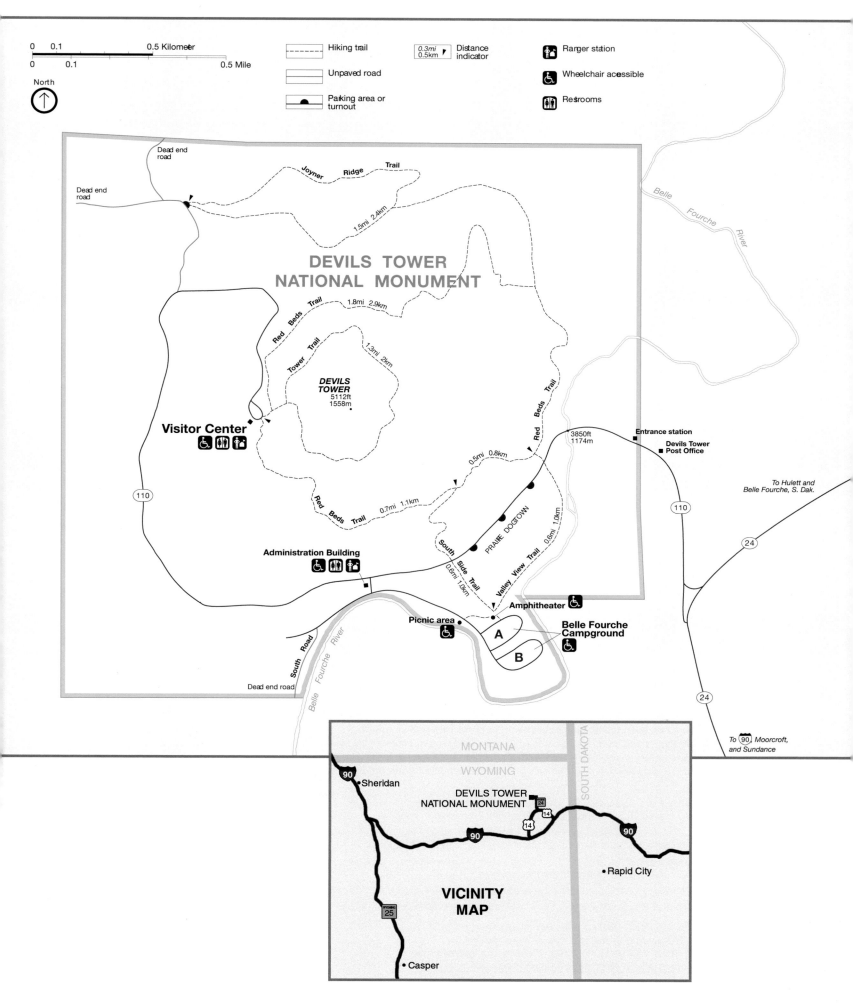

Scale and Legend

0   0.1   0.5 Kilometer
0   0.1   0.5 Mile

North

- - - - Hiking trail

Unpaved road

Parking area or turnout

0.3mi / 0.5km Distance indicator

Ranger station

Wheelchair accessible

Restrooms

DEVILS TOWER NATIONAL MONUMENT

Dead end road

Dead end road

Joyner Ridge Trail

1.5mi 2.4km

Red Beds Trail

1.8mi 2.9km

Tower Trail

1.3mi 2km

DEVILS TOWER
5112ft
1558m

Visitor Center

Red Beds Trail

0.5mi 0.8km

3850ft
1174m

Entrance station

Devils Tower Post Office

110

Red Beds Trail

0.7mi 1.1km

PRAIRIE DOGTOWN

South Side Trail

0.6mi 1.0km

Valley View Trail

0.6mi 1.0km

Administration Building

Amphitheater

Picnic area

A

B

Belle Fourche Campground

South Road

Belle Fourche River

Dead end road

110

24

To Hulett and Belle Fourche, S. Dak.

24

To 90 Moorcroft, and Sundance

VICINITY MAP

MONTANA
WYOMING

SOUTH DAKOTA

90
•Sheridan

DEVILS TOWER NATIONAL MONUMENT

24
14
14

90

90

• Rapid City

WYOMING 25

• Casper

Devils Tower to the Future

CATHERINE GOCKLEY

You think rock can't bend? As magma it exists in a fluid state for us to see millions of years later.

But let's not have these human events blind us from the true story of the Tower. The hands of Mother Nature have carved a magnificent sculpture, and she continues to alter it. Perhaps in our lifetime, another column will come crashing down revealing a new line of age in the Tower's face.

It has been around for some 50 million years, and we are entrusted to preserve the Tower and the surrounding Black Hills. The proper management of the 1,347 acres of park grounds is delegated to the superintendent and park staff; but the sheer experience of the entire area, litter free and clear of the smog and waste that contaminates much of our country, is up to all of us.

Protecting nature's true playground with the loping deer, the straight, ponderosa pines, and the vibrant hues of red and gold will ensure another 50 million years of wonder and spectacle. Though eventually, Nature's hand may whittle Devils Tower to a needle of towering rock, the work will be hers and will evoke a new type of awe for generations to come.

KC Publications has been the leading publisher of colorful, interpretive books about National Park areas, public lands, Indian Culture, and related subjects for over 45 years. We have 5 active series – over 125 titles – with Translation Packages in up to 8 languages for over half the areas we cover.   Write, call, or visit our web site for our full-color catalog.

Our series are:

The Story Behind the Scenery® – Compelling stories of over 65 National Park areas and similar Public Land areas. Some with Translation Packages.

in pictures... Nature's Continuing Story®– A companion, pictorially oriented, series on America's National Parks.   All titles have Translation Packages.

For Young Adventurers® – Dedicated to young seekers and keepers of all things wild and sacred. Explore America's Heritage from A to Z.

Voyage of Discovery® – Exploration of the expansion of the western United States.

Indian Culture and the Southwest – All about Native Americans, past and present.

We publish over 125 titles – Books and other related specialty products.
   Our full-color catalog is available online or by contacting us:
Call (800) 626-9673, Fax (928) 684-5189, Write to the address below,
   Or visit our web site at www.nationalparksbooks.com

Published by KC Publications • P.O. Box 3615 • Wickenburg, AZ 85358

Inside back cover: The white-tailed deer forage for uncovered grasses in winter. Photo by Wes Carroll.

Back cover: One final view of the Tower's polygonal (many-sided) columns. Photo by Jeff Gnass.

Created, Designed, and Published in the U.S.A.
Printed by Tien Wah Press (Pte.) Ltd, Singapore
Pre-Press by United Graphic Pte. Ltd